The Creation, The Fall And The Promise

Written by Joshua J. Radke

Illustrated by Kelly Irene Schumacher

GRAIL QUEST BOOKS + BANGOR

PUBLISHER
Kasandra M. Radke

COVER ILLUSTRATION
Kelly Irene Schumacher

LAYOUT DESIGN
Ryan Porter

PUBLICATION HISTORY
Paperback edition/September 2017

PRINTED IN THE UNITED STATES OF AMERICA
157908642

Grail Quest Books can be found online at
http://www.grailquestbooks.com

For more work by Kelly Irene Schumacher, please visit
http://agnusdeiarts.com

Some parts of this book were inspired by elements of the Blessed Martin Luther's lectures on Genesis, as well as several sermons of Lutheran pastor, Valerius Herberger (1562-1627), translated by Mr Matthew Carver for *The Great Works of God Part One and Two: The Mysteries of Christ in The Book of Genesis, Chapter 1-15* (Concordia Publishing House, 2010).

The Authour would also like to thank Rev Samuel Schuldheisz for graciously looking over the manuscript, especially the theological matter, and Mr Ryan Porter for employing his many technical talents towards putting all the various parts of the book together. Thank you also to those contributing to various aspects of this project be it pointing out some unclear prose, affirming art concepts, helping to tell folks about the book ahead of publication, et al: Rev Jonathan Fisk, Rev Paul Schulz, Rev Richard Juritsch, Mr Eric Postma, Mr Peter Slayton. Thank you to my wife, Kasandra, and Rev Tyrel Bramwell, Rev Gaven Mize, and Rev Christopher Thoma for vital encouragement along the way.

Finally, I would like to thank the incredibly gifted Artist, Ms Kelly Schumacher: the Word of God is visually captivating, working the imagination. Kelly's illustrations bring to life the words I have written in ways that have surpassed any expectation I could have fathomed. Her art for this book has taught me and edified me in the beauty of the Faith, being one of the essential functions of the LORD's gift of Art to His creation.

Deo gratias.

DEDICATION
To the meek, made pure in heart as they are prepared to inherit
the Kingdom to come in Christ, for they shall behold God for eternity.

ARTIST'S DEDICATION

To Mom & Dad

In the beginning was The Word of GOD. He would be born as the Light of men: Jesus—truly GOD, truly a man. GOD decided, even before anything was created, that all who believed in Jesus would be graciously saved from sin (which we brought into Creation), to live with GOD forever.

And in the beginning GOD made the heavens and earth: there was nothing else, except darkness and GOD:

GOD the Father—the Master Creator, providing all things.
GOD the Son—the Master Craftsman, by His Word.
GOD the Spirit—the Master Life-giver, brooding over creation.

GOD said "Let there be light." Out of the dark 'nothing' came the light. Perhaps this light was not as bright as the sun would be; it probably was not nearly as bright as the Divine Light that illumines all things, which we will see when GOD creates the new sinless heavens and earth when Jesus returns on the Last Day. But to GOD this first light was good.

This was Sunday.

GOD also creates something out of nothing when He creates faith, by the Light of His Word, from the dark nothing of our sinfulness. Only through the gracious miracle of faith in Jesus, by His death and resurrection, GOD says: 'You are good.'

uch things are mysteries we cannot understand, but we believe them because Jesus says they are true.

GOD said: "Let the water above separate from the water below." The air expanded and this was done. The waters in the sky were gathered into clouds, which brings us the rain and snow. This was Monday.

The Word that keeps the waters firmly separated by the sky is the same Word that has promised that nothing in creation—not even death—shall be able to separate us from the love of GOD, thanks to our LORD Jesus, to Whom we are connected in Baptism.

GOD said: "Let the waters under the sky come together; let the dry land be seen." The waters obeyed His command and became oceans, seas, lakes, rivers, ponds, and streams. The dry land that appeared GOD named 'Earth'. In His eyes, this was good.

Isn't it interesting that the Earth, which would be used by GOD to form man, came out of the water by The Word of GOD?

This reminds us of our Baptism, when we come out of water by The Word as new creations in Jesus!

GOD said: "Let there be plants and trees with fruit, and seeds to produce more trees and fruit." There were no seasons yet, and so the grass, and flowers, and fruit trees grew as GOD had commanded. These were good in the sight of GOD. This was Tuesday.

On this day of creation we think about the seeds GOD planted and produced to be eaten. GOD plants and waters seeds of faith in us through His Word so that we will produce fruits of love for our family and friends at church, in school, at home, and in our chores.

GOD knew that one day one of the trees He created would be cut down and made into a cross. His Son, Jesus, would have to die on that piece of wood because of our sins. He would be buried in the Earth, and be raised to life—like a flower after the cold dead of winter.

This day of creation also reminds us of a verse from a hymn, 'O Come, O Come, Emmanuel,' which was written a long time ago about Jesus. We sing it at Christmas time; one of the verses describes Jesus as being the Branch from the royal family tree of Jesse, the father of King David, Who will free us from the devil and save us from the grave.

OD said: "Let there be a great light for the day, and a lesser light for the night." From this command, the sun and moon were created. GOD also knew that these lights would be useful to help life grow on Earth; also to know the time, and the day of the month.

Like the sun, Jesus chases away the dark storm clouds of life that make us afraid or sad. Like the moon, we receive His Light and reflect it to other people who need to know Jesus is with them and forgives them.

OD also created the stars and other planets on this day. GOD knew these heavenly bodies would help us to know the seasons and where we are on the Earth when we travel. They also make the night sky beautiful. This was Wednesday.

ur enchantment with the heavens beyond Earth, and the magic of fairy tales and stories that take place on other worlds, are ways GOD reminds us we are made for the new heaven and new Earth that will come when Jesus returns for us.

GOD had plans to use all these heavenly bodies in miracles to show all people His power and authority. They would also play important roles in announcing the birth of His Son, Jesus, as well as the death of Jesus on the cross for our sins, so that for His sake we will live forever with Him!

OD said: "Let living animals come from the waters, to fill the waters and the air." And according to His will, The Word created from the water the fish, the whales, the dragons, and all the creatures of the waters; also doves, ravens, roosters, hens, and all the birds.

Like a pelican providing food and protection with her two wings, GOD the Father provides for us according to His will through His mighty Word of Promise in your Baptism, the LORD's Supper, and when the pastor says, "In the Name of + Jesus, I forgive you." He protects us by strengthening our faith whenever we hear His Word in the Law and the Gospel.

OD saw that the fish and birds He had made were good. Then He put a blessing on them all to produce living creatures like itself, and to grow in number. This was Thursday.

When we wish someone well it is because we want nice things for them, but we have no power to make this happen. The Word of GOD, which created everything in the universe, does have this power! GOD wants us to ask Him through prayer in Jesus' Name to provide our family and friends good things, according to His gracious will.

GOD said: "Let living animals come from the Earth." And according to His will The Word created from the Earth all the creatures that walk on land—such as lions, bears, donkeys, foxes, sheep, cats, dogs, and horses (although they did not have these names yet).

Sheep and lambs have a very important role in GOD's creation. Jesus calls us His beloved sheep, and He is our Shepherd bearing the rod and staff in love. Also, sometimes at church we sing a song that talks about Jesus: "Worthy is Christ, the Lamb Who was slain, whose blood set us free to be people of GOD."

GOD said: "Let Us create man in our image. They shall rule over the animals in the waters and on the Earth." The LORD Hand-crafted the first man from the dust of the Earth. GOD breathed into the man His breath of life; the man was now a living person.

In Baptism you are made a new creation in Jesus by GOD, through His Word! And just as He named this personally made creature, "man" (or Adam—which means 'from the Earth'), GOD gives you His own Name when the pastor baptizes you "in the Name of the Father, and of the + Son, and of the Holy Spirit."

The Life-giving Holy Spirit is breathed into you by The Word, and you receive GOD's promise of everlasting life through faith in Christ Jesus.

GOD planted a wonderful garden in the country called Eden. A river came from Eden and split into four smaller rivers to water the garden, which was called Paradise.

These rivers remind us of Jesus and His Word. Jesus is the primary source of "living water". This "water" refreshes us when we "drink" from it—that is when we hear and study GOD's Word and are reminded of His Gospel promises. This Gospel flows from Jesus to all four directions on the Earth—north, south, east, west.

This "living water" of the Word waters the seeds of our faith to grow into trees bearing fruit for the good of our neighbor and the glory of God.

Into this garden GOD placed Adam, and made beautiful trees that produced good food—including two very special trees.

God wanted Adam to care for this garden, to act as a kind of high priest over it. This was his vocation (which means 'a calling' to do a specific kind of job).

GOD said that Adam could eat the fruit from almost every tree in Paradise. This included one of the special trees that preserved immortal Life; meaning this tree would keep Adam strong and healthy, and allow him to stay young forever, which is the will of GOD for mankind.

The one tree from which Adam could not eat was the tree GOD had created to be a special sanctuary, where man was to worship GOD and hear His Word. The fruit on this tree was very good, but eating it would cause Adam to suffer death—because Adam would be disobeying GOD's Word by eating the fruit. GOD's command was intended to be how Adam would worship GOD in perfect obedience and praise.

THE PARADE FOR ALPACAS

By Robyn Tunley

Title: The Parade for Alpacas
Author: Robyn Tunley
Illustrations by: Robyn Tunley
Published by: Robyn's Nest LLC
Publication date: 07/11/2023

ISBN: 9798851934421
For inquiries, please contact: Robyn's Nest LLC
Email: betteryourself.robynsnestllc@gmail.com

Printed in the United State of America

The Parade for Alpacas

Written and Illustrated by
Robyn Tunley

This book is dedicated to My Husband and my two children, for always supporting me.
Also, to my father, who keeps introducing me to new challenges and keeping me inspired to keep trying new things.

Once upon a time, on a cozy alpaca farm nestled in the rolling hills, there lived a lively group of alpacas.

There were fluffy white alpacas, spotty brown alpacas, and even some alpacas with colorful coats. They were the best of friends and loved to explore and play together every day.

One sunny morning, as the alpacas were munching on their breakfast, they heard a strange noise coming from the distance.

Curious as can be, they looked up and saw a big crowd of people walking towards their farm.

"Look, look!" exclaimed Alfie, the mischievous alpaca with a brown and white coat. "It's a grand parade just for us!"

The alpacas lined up near the gate, eagerly waiting for the parade to arrive. They were so excited, their hooves started to tap-dance on the grass!

First came a tall man with a bushy beard
and a curly mustache. The alpacas
giggled, thinking he looked like a
friendly mountain goat.

10

Next came a woman wearing a bright red hat with feathers sticking out. The alpacas thought she looked like a tropical bird, ready to take flight!

Then, a little girl skipped by, wearing rainbow-colored shoes and a shirt covered in sparkles. The alpacas thought she looked like a magical unicorn!

   As the parade continued, the alpacas saw people of all shapes, sizes, and colors. Some had glasses, some had curly hair, and some even had tattoos. It was a colorful and diverse group indeed!

The alpacas realized that each person in the parade was unique in their own special way. They learned that just like them, people can come in all different shapes, sizes, and colors.

The alpacas knew it was important to embrace these differences. So, they decided to welcome each person with open hearts and kind smiles.

As the parade came to an end, the alpacas thanked each person for making their day so special. They were grateful for the diversity they had witnessed and made new friends along the way.

The alpacas understood that embracing
differences and treating everyone with
kindness made the world a happier
place. From that day forward, they
greeted every visitor with warmth and
love.

And so, the alpacas lived happily ever after, always remembering the grand parade that taught them about diversity and acceptance. The End.

Please feel free to make your own
Alpaca friends. Color each picture. Give
them a name.

Name:

_____

_____

Name:

_____

_____

Name:

_____

_____

Name:

_____

_____

Name:

_____

_____

Name:

_____

_____

Name:

_____

_____

Made in the USA
Coppell, TX
21 September 2023

21841015R00017

GOD saw that Adam was alone, and this was not good. GOD caused all the animals to come to Adam, for him to give them a name—like "donkey" or "eagle"—and to find a helper. But there was no animal right for him.

So GOD caused Adam to fall into a deep sleep. GOD took a rib from Adam's side and created a female. Because she had been created from Adam's bone and flesh, Adam called her "woman", which means 'out of man'.

The creation of the woman reminds us of how Jesus "fell asleep" in death on the cross, and was wounded in His side. Water and blood came from the wound: by Baptism we become children of GOD, and by His Blood in the Lord's Supper our faith is fed. By these Sacraments, the church is created; the Church is considered the "bride of Christ".

OD blessed man and woman (which was the first marriage) and all the animals on the Earth: "Be fruitful and multiply and fill the Earth and tame it and rule over the fish and birds and every living thing that moves on the Earth." And GOD saw that all was very good. This was Friday, and GOD's work was finished.

And on Saturday, GOD rested from all His good work.

n Good Friday, GOD, in the Person of our Saviour, Jesus, finished His work of redeeming all mankind from its sin.

He was placed in the tomb, and on Holy Saturday, Christ rested.

The serpent was part of the creation that GOD called "good", and its nature was to be crafty. This suited our enemy, the devil. While GOD rested from all His work, the devil took on the form of this creature and tempted the woman to doubt GOD's Word by asking, "Did GOD really say…?" The devil was an angel that GOD created good, but he decided to despise GOD and do evil, such as ruin GOD's Creation.

The devil is always tempting us to doubt GOD's Word, especially all the good things that GOD has promised us through faith and prayer in Jesus. The devil tempts us to listen to what he wants us to hear through many voices in the world which do not believe GOD; he would have us make decisions using the "inner voice" of our thoughts and emotions. The devil would have us believe that we do not receive forgiveness for our sins in Holy Baptism, or that Jesus is not truly present in the bread and wine of Holy Communion, or that confessing your sins to your pastor is too embarrassing and does not help.

The devil is wrong; Jesus says he is a liar.

Deceived by the devil that GOD was not good, had not given them everything they needed, and that GOD was lying about the punishment of death for not obeying His Word, the woman ate the fruit of the tree. Her husband, Adam, allowed this sin to take place, and then decided to also sin by taking the fruit offered to him by his wife and eating of it.

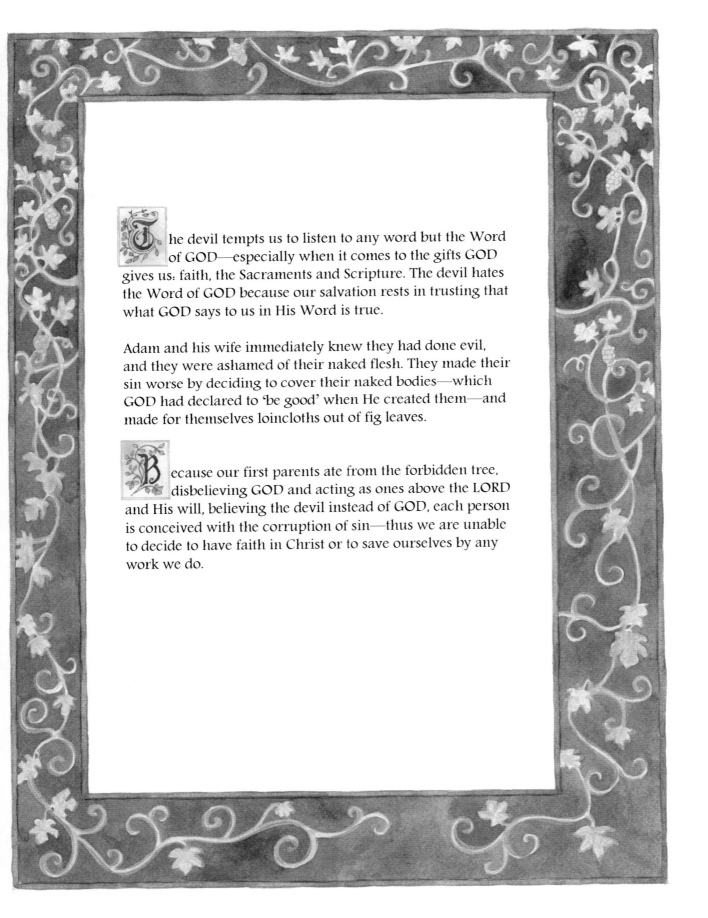

The devil tempts us to listen to any word but the Word of GOD—especially when it comes to the gifts GOD gives us: faith, the Sacraments and Scripture. The devil hates the Word of GOD because our salvation rests in trusting that what GOD says to us in His Word is true.

Adam and his wife immediately knew they had done evil, and they were ashamed of their naked flesh. They made their sin worse by deciding to cover their naked bodies—which GOD had declared to 'be good' when He created them—and made for themselves loincloths out of fig leaves.

Because our first parents ate from the forbidden tree, disbelieving GOD and acting as ones above the LORD and His will, believing the devil instead of GOD, each person is conceived with the corruption of sin—thus we are unable to decide to have faith in Christ or to save ourselves by any work we do.

On Sunday, the eighth day of the world, GOD was walking through Paradise. The man and woman heard the Voice of the LORD, and were afraid. So they hid themselves from the Face of the LORD GOD.

Adam and his wife had never feared the Voice of the LORD in this manner before. And yet now, knowing the evil they have done, they are terrified of GOD and despair. They hide themselves, even in the bright light of the day, believing they can somehow escape GOD's anger and judgment. This is how sin works: one sin makes more sins. It results in foolish behaviour, especially the belief that we can somehow hide from our LORD.

Then GOD called for Adam: "Where are you?" And Adam responded that he had been afraid when he heard the LORD's Voice and hid himself because he was naked. GOD asked Adam who had revealed that he was naked, and if Adam had eaten of the forbidden tree. Adam admitted that he did eat of the tree, but blamed the woman GOD had given him for his sin; the woman blamed the serpent (that is, the devil) for deceiving her.

We are just like Adam and his wife. When we realize we have done wrong—either against GOD or against someone in our life—we often attempt to cover our sin by making a lie. When someone comes who we know will reveal our sin against GOD or another person, we try to hide. When we are forced to face the sin, we blame other people and even GOD Himself—we even try to defend our sinful actions.

We must confess our sins, to GOD and to the person we have sinned against. GOD has given us the great blessing of pastors to help us confess our sins, and to repent.

The LORD GOD turned to the serpent and cursed it with a life of permanent submission and dust. Then to the devil, who is already condemned for his rebellion against GOD in heaven, He pronounces the severest punishment any creature can receive: the promise of defeat without mercy.

"There shall be hatred between you and the woman, and between your seed and her Seed. He shall crush your head, and you will strike His heel."

The words GOD speaks to the devil are for the benefit of Adam and the woman—indeed all of creation. The devil brought death and destruction to GOD's good work, but the LORD promises the devil will be crushed for his evil.

The Seed of the woman is Christ Jesus, our LORD, and He shall destroy the devil, death, and sin forever. It is important to note that GOD said it would be only the Seed of woman who could defeat the devil and his evil: the work of salvation is completely outside of our power; it is only GOD's work. Moreover, the fate of the devil would come by way of woman—the very creature he deceived. Thus Adam and his wife, sunk deep in their sin for breaking GOD's Holy Law, have received Good News: the Gospel.

Just like the serpent, Adam and his wife will bear curses for the rest of their lives, which will affect all mankind and creation.

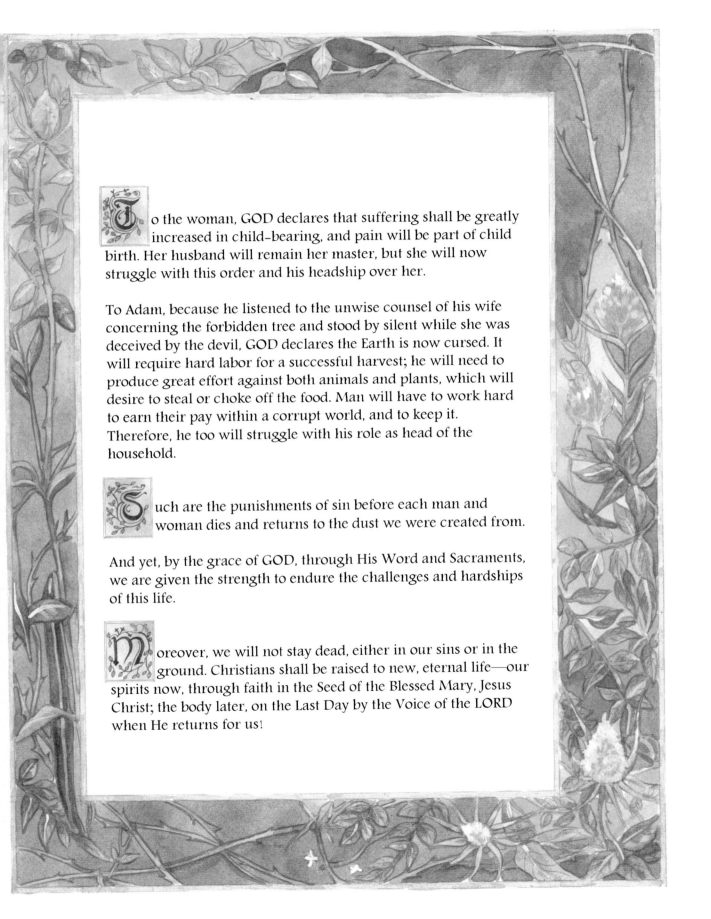

To the woman, GOD declares that suffering shall be greatly increased in child-bearing, and pain will be part of child birth. Her husband will remain her master, but she will now struggle with this order and his headship over her.

To Adam, because he listened to the unwise counsel of his wife concerning the forbidden tree and stood by silent while she was deceived by the devil, GOD declares the Earth is now cursed. It will require hard labor for a successful harvest; he will need to produce great effort against both animals and plants, which will desire to steal or choke off the food. Man will have to work hard to earn their pay within a corrupt world, and to keep it. Therefore, he too will struggle with his role as head of the household.

Such are the punishments of sin before each man and woman dies and returns to the dust we were created from.

And yet, by the grace of GOD, through His Word and Sacraments, we are given the strength to endure the challenges and hardships of this life.

Moreover, we will not stay dead, either in our sins or in the ground. Christians shall be raised to new, eternal life—our spirits now, through faith in the Seed of the Blessed Mary, Jesus Christ; the body later, on the Last Day by the Voice of the LORD when He returns for us!

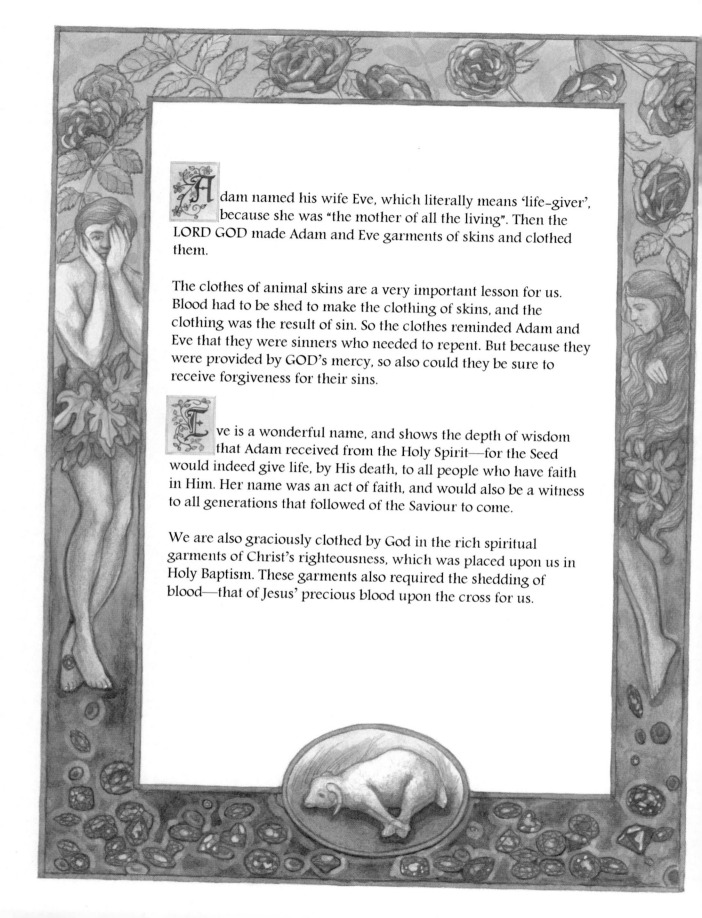

Adam named his wife Eve, which literally means 'life-giver', because she was "the mother of all the living". Then the LORD GOD made Adam and Eve garments of skins and clothed them.

The clothes of animal skins are a very important lesson for us. Blood had to be shed to make the clothing of skins, and the clothing was the result of sin. So the clothes reminded Adam and Eve that they were sinners who needed to repent. But because they were provided by GOD's mercy, so also could they be sure to receive forgiveness for their sins.

Eve is a wonderful name, and shows the depth of wisdom that Adam received from the Holy Spirit—for the Seed would indeed give life, by His death, to all people who have faith in Him. Her name was an act of faith, and would also be a witness to all generations that followed of the Saviour to come.

We are also graciously clothed by God in the rich spiritual garments of Christ's righteousness, which was placed upon us in Holy Baptism. These garments also required the shedding of blood—that of Jesus' precious blood upon the cross for us.

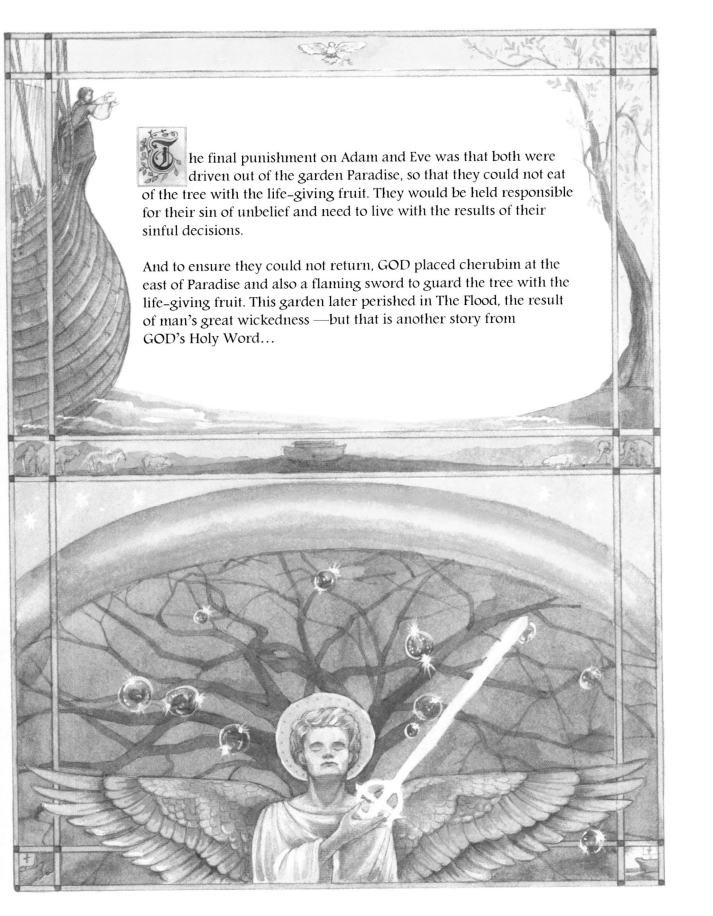

The final punishment on Adam and Eve was that both were driven out of the garden Paradise, so that they could not eat of the tree with the life-giving fruit. They would be held responsible for their sin of unbelief and need to live with the results of their sinful decisions.

And to ensure they could not return, GOD placed cherubim at the east of Paradise and also a flaming sword to guard the tree with the life-giving fruit. This garden later perished in The Flood, the result of man's great wickedness —but that is another story from GOD's Holy Word...

Our "Tree of Life" is His cross, and its "food" is Jesus Himself, whose Body and Blood we receive in the Lord's Supper. By His death on that tree of perfect obedience, the flaming sword of GOD's wrath retreats, allowing us to receive this Tree's blessed Fruit of Life. This food keeps us strong and healthy in a spiritual way by strengthening our faith, forgiving our sins, and preserving in us the hope of eternal life that God has promised, thanks to our Baptism in Jesus. This is all a mystery, which is why we call Holy Communion and Holy Baptism sacraments (which means 'sacred mysteries').

Truly, this day, by faith in Christ and His Holy Word, you are with Jesus in Paradise. And when He returns, and brings with Him the new creation and new Paradise, the Tree of Life that was given to our first parents will again welcome GOD's people to receive its good and abundant fruit.

And we shall reign with the Lord GOD forever and ever.

In the Name + of Jesus: Amen.

Made in the USA
Coppell, TX
21 September 2023

21845993R00031